Ecclesiastes

Rare Wisdom Versed

Uche Kezborn

authorHOUSE®

AuthorHouse™ UK Ltd.
500 Avebury Boulevard
Central Milton Keynes, MK9 2BE
www.authorhouse.co.uk
Phone: 08001974150

First published by AuthorHouse 5/10/2010

ISBN: 978-1-4490-8688-6 (sc)

This book is printed on acid-free paper.

Dedicated to my family and all who believe in me, gave me hope and have been saying "you can" when all hope seemed lost.

I love you all.

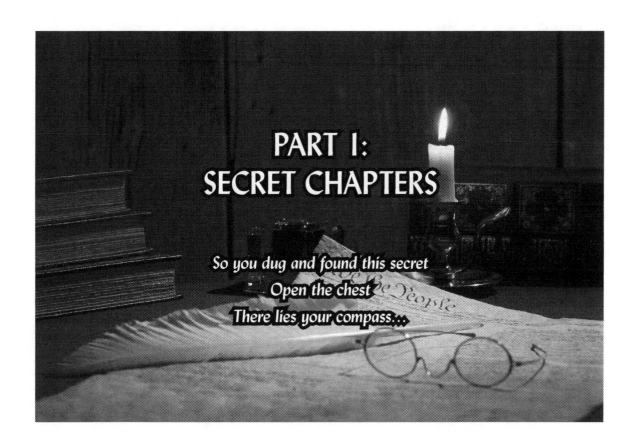

PART 1:
SECRET CHAPTERS

So you dug and found this secret
Open the chest
There lies your compass...

PRIDE OF INK

Liquid

Caged

And let out through a point

Ideas flow

Imagination registers

Dots on paper

For consumption

Equipment and direction

All hail the conveyer

When minds were fed

Echoes of the stunned

Hands-swaying

Of the captivated; or

Plaques added to laurels

Whichever way appraisal comes?

That's the pride of ink

DRAWERS OF INK

Without the powers of reality

Clairvoyants would not convince

That liquid could speak

With the voices that could;

Build or pull or destroy

Liquid: mostly with

The color of peace and boldness

Pouring to make or, to mar

Dropping on the plain

The message to inform, educate and alert

Through the veins of the ink

Flows new life

The conscience; guiding the misguided

Moulding unsaid words

Setting principles to life

Continually, creating new words

A DAY WITHOUT HIS PEN

Walking down a sub-way

A dip in the left hip pocket

Wasn't reassuring as afore

He wondered what would be done

In the safe house

He talked to one less than

Half a dozen of mixed genders

In the search of finger printer

Before now

He'd wanted to scribble

The acts of players in the abstract

Rolling in as inspirations

Buyers waited

As his neighbor guarantee

They get "inner voices"

Whenever he says; "your pen please"

Characterized by unusual but

New things with positive signs

Perseverance paid the result

Seeming "disappointment" offered

Direction to a vision

Finding a reason to smile

And be happy again... he vowed

... To write along,

Picking reasons to write

In the last times of the day

He couldn't write with borrowed ink

And the words hover within

He loved the day

Day without his pen

On it was drawn the blue-print of his days

His pen was with… Eve from the last evening

To write the affection statement

SPROUTING BUD

Like the sprouting bud

Pierces through the earth;

To feel the spark of the sun

Like a bride

Anticipates the touch of aisle floor

To answer a groom's name

    Unheard voice beckons for a spectrum

    From where to speak.

    Among the drawers of ink,

    An inked brush sways to paint

    The beauty of perfection

Grant, permit, allow-

The fronds to weave

The mason to mix mortar

The rhythm to rhyme

    And the bud sprouts

    From tender leaves to stems of trunk

    Leaves- evergreen and a shield

BLUE PRINT

A call have been made

There are no signs to convey it through

For assumption perceives no deaf

We are all here as actors

There are no seats for spectators though

For the world is made a personalized stage

Where each act plays individually

 Who are these? - Watching and jubilating

'Should be working on your blue print

.

CANNED STAR

In the obscurity

Lies numerous potentials

Talents unused

Unplanted seeds

Who could?

Risk uncorking the can

Afford to trade the talents

Lease his land to the seeds

Let the rains give way

To the bright cloud

The bright cloud

On which stars spark and shines

THE LAY MAN

He may have ideas though

When there is no drive

Dreams die

He walks around

A mobile cemetery

On its tomb lay unused ideas

An offering of a hand

That which have been dead

Would be caught up in the sky

- Where stars live

UNLUCKY MAN

Forces or fate?

Many sides unequal

Attributes to a fair die

A hand tosses and get single

And another yet, gets the value

Of the entire sides

Differences; in the toss

Or in the die?

Or are there forces that sway beneath?

BARREN LAND

Of? Fate

Predestination

Providence

Self will

Circumstances

Time, chance and seasons

The weak lay blames

The eluded cast spears

The favored has stakes in boast

The heart that has not known

Wait... be curious

Eagerly, search

Don't lay blames

Cast no spears!

Sell your shares

Every heart will witness

The confused cleared

When miners become champions

Bring out your eyes

Is the earth cursed?

Then God must be a liar

But... can Truth lie?

Part 1: Secret Chapters

Before the seventh day

All creation were endorsed as good

Bring out your eyes

Look around

Get busy

Mine gradually... consistently

Till each explorer

Owns a stake in nature's treasury

SIGHTS OF DESPAIR

Where will I lay?

Ideas die at conception

For the materials are still raw

Alone

Hope seem to have no hook

Anchor had disappointed

Look behind

Be an unbeliever of its failures

Measure not with its ruler

The sizes encompasses

The heights not reached

Goals not achieved

Ideas aborted

FADED JOY

Oh that... hmm!

If I could make a request

How pleasant it will be to demise

Since the moments longed for

Seem to disappear

At almost grab

'Never thought it could be denial

How suddenly an anticipated joy

Became trunk of worries

That cannot be easily forgotten

Even with forced smiles

It wakes with the dawn

Struck with uneasiness

Weakness, disgust went down my spine

My heart is trodden with this feel

Like a gift of rose

Trampled before the beneficiary

When it is about to be delivered

Then my whole system dampen

Weariness became my closet pal

My delight and joy seem to turn worries

Though it will last for sure

I'm confident it is for a moment

Then an overwhelming joy emerges

SEAT OF WORRIES

Locked up by circumstances

And made the gate man

In the Island of uncertainty

The foolishness of dreams

The vain of wishes

The beauty of fantasy

The man sat on convenience

A prisoner of self

Yet the key holder

DREAMS

What a world

With tourist attractions

Calling human to visit

And multiply the sight of their minds

A diviner

Seeing the positive and negative tomorrow

In black-and-white and colored

Often times the predictions come true

An imaginary phenomenon

Where wishes never run dry

Building hopes like Babel

And castles in the air

Their killers shed no blood

Giving the victims poisoned vinegar

Intoxicated with hopes and

Call gamblers ticket an asset

It's the world of creation

Where anxious minds were taught

The sign of regulations and unmade things

To relay to the common man

GAMBLERS' TICKET

Wishes are real

As expectation exists

If they were fortunes;

The world would have been no less than

Kings and princes paradise

Housing no destitute

Dream dreams

Toss target

Plant purpose

Welcome wishes,

While they whisper at you

Feel-for-free are their price tag

Buy wishes a real estate

Adorn dreams like apparel

When desire lies on the broker's public offer list:

Disappointment, anguish, loss of hope

Could inhabit the once optimistic mind

That keeps a gambler ticket as an asset

FAILURES' LODGE

Go by that name

And success would mourn

And scorn at you

Their avenue lay desolate

Like the streets at church hours

Sympathizers are scoffers

The novercals of woe

No joy

All daylong their garments are woes

And worries are their embrace

Their walls are tiles of mongers

Eavesdropped from the chants of blame

Live here

And you'll feel

As the one adorned with a turn coat

They would assume

The spats of toddler princes

For drizzles of dews

EMPTY WALLET

Optimism could obliterate

Desires are damaged

Anticipations would be antagonized

As stiff and still as breathless being

The life with pocket-less attire

Like the burnt-bundle of tied notes

The hope of unrealized dreams

Thought would wander

Mind could create

Ideas informed

The taste of reality

Leans on the spirit of dead heroes

Immortalized on rectangular papers

Endorsed by the living signature

FANTASY LAND

No barriers

To what could be thought

No restrictions

To all that could be cherished

The highway to wishes;

A straight road

With the end in view

Most dwellers

Never exist in reality, still

Everything seem possible

Here

Beggars ride on horses

Princes assume the Almighty

Kings dethrone gods

Most dwellers

Never exist in reality. Still

Everything seem possible

DREAMER

Get out of bed

If you must tell the tale

Perhaps;

Of how the desert were estate

Of how mortar were made bricks

Of how the sea partitioned dry land

Of how paupers were princes

Get busy

If there would be realization

Perhaps:

Of how proposals were endorsed

Of ideas materialized

Of fantasy fertilized

Of wishes granted

PEOPLE!

Discovery on time

Would save some breath

And keep you to the next moment

Though you lay in their coma

Accept their praises

Don't sit on their adoration

Their seats are framed magnificence

Eaten by maggots

Insatiable...

Trial for their satisfaction

Is as good as beating an egg

Broken on the soil

PEOPLES' OPINION

If it is a white Cain

The world would lack

The visually impaired; consequently

From their false guide perhaps

Hold the cock by the feather

Their opinion

Would wish it were by the legs

Catch the dog by the neck

Their suggestion

Could opine it were by the paw

Their followers

Assume the traits of the inhabitants

Of Gaga land

Actors of the scenes of confusion

COULD YOU WAIT?

Though ways seem crooked

The measure of burden seem to

Outweigh the grace of hope

Troubles on every side

Sways faith like feathers

No matter hard the trials and

Persistent the perspiration

In the end though

The means seem unjustified

Like the tick of seconds

Is the count of seasons

Times are strictly guided by regulation

If wishes were as real as facts

The orb would not be partitioned by class

Assumptions could blow like barroom

Little longer the air is dispersed

In the weight of time

Adorn patience

PART 2: RELATIONSHIP X-RAY

It' power rules beings inhuman
How much more would it to humans
When their affection is diagnosed

DIVAS' HEART

Fragile, fra-gi-le, frag... fragile!

Handle with care

If eventually broken

There had been cracks of brokenness

Like a pilgrim

She tours and settles on any flourishing ambience

When the green fade, they relocate

Flirting, she flies like a butterfly-

That continually perches on diverse petals

Can't the woman stay?

To discover the truth in promise

Her heart is not constant, though

Still the constant philosophy transforms her

Like a wax

She melts at flame contact

An air time PIN;

Available for subscribers to scratch

The heart of women!

A ROSE IN THE DEW

Positioning so soothing

Palatable; the flies' feels

The fragrance of her beauty

The dew, her mould

The dawn announces her pleasant mien

At dawn the dew drizzles into her

Till the east feel the heat

Flies endured the form of the flower

Only to disappear at the scorch feel

When the leaves shrink and whither

The eyes desire the one with beautiful wings

The fly perched for the flowers fragrance

REPEATED WORDS

From afar though,

I clearly heard the sounds of babbling

From the vast trampling feet

Resistance could not shut the ears

Nor cease their words

As different face of genders

Meet from opposite direction

Fluency stammers her speeches repeatedly

The foot misses steps. Though

But more resounding

The appeal for attention

Confusion had observed this act

On diverse scenarios though,

And the real senses of these signs were a wonder.

The quartet-word with blood complexion assures:

It is the fore-runner of availability clause

That validates the signs of the unspoken words

Of dying feelings and

Lonely emotions calling:

If you could be willing,

I am available

Talk to me, please

AWAKE

All nightlong

Within the nature's generation:

The gentle breeze,

The randomly whisked sounds of the birds,

The dead rest of the waters,

The purple star-studded clouds,

The 'gentle' snores from among the few

Of all that lay

Within the dark clouded room

Beside a gender fit for discrimination,

Fit for embrace at such setting

Signs hover all around

As the cloud is above the earth

Mind could not interpret the sign' reality

As each lay opposite the other

Absent from nature's call register

Owing the impulse- unrelated

The question of unanswered signs

Still the eyes were blind

As each lay awake... laying still

In fragility through the distant night

Dizzy at dawn, they...

... Slept

IDOL WORSHIPPERS

Sitting at the gate at eve

Beating the rhythm of the wind

Hearing whispers from afar;

Of nature and its inhabitants

Suddenly there was a flash

From the face as goddess

Of beautiful flowing river

Necks crack and screw and giraffe-

To capture a glimpse of the flash

Admiring in paparazzi pose

While they snap and print and save... in memory

Their hearts are far island restricted

To have visited though

Mine suggest what happens in other lands:

Adoration and reverence and obeisance-

To the flash

Admiration affirms the mind of these eyes

Have bowed before this beauty

Of the diva

THROW THE CAGE WIDE OPEN

Conservation covers concern

Possessiveness prides partnership

Their scepter forbids

The subject even

To wave at compatriots in king presence

Cage may not be for birds

Till there came an itching ear

That yearns for soft rhythm

Throw the cage open...

If you caught a bird

The surrounded-open-city

May subject their die-hards to survive

Open the cage gate

Though she flee away

Shut not the gate against them

While they return

The prodigal song lyrics; "I am home"

If the cage swings empty,

Reset eyes up to the green

The former don't deserve your ambience

ALONE

Away from companions

Keenly kept from family

Love and friends

Who would have thought?

An entity with much surrounding

Will be all that alone

It's the souls envelope that

Could only be found around

But we are one all the same

Cause I'm filled with quietness of dawn

Like the isles

When loneliness answers the questions

I'm faced with outside abroad

Who would draw near?

To take the arm and

Break the long silence

How would there be loneliness?

Where love, friends and companion abounds

Take my hand... I feel you

DIVAS' MIGHT

When the subtracted adds herself;

The denied equips but self

Mighty fall

Weak toll

While in strength search

Lest marginalization empower her

Like a colossus she positions

Above the panthers

When they patronize

The in-built might that instills

Strength in a weaker vessel, thus:

Defeating the strong

And humiliating the mighty

STRENGHT OF THE WEAK

Made with one out of many

Formed outside creation days

After the creator had rested

Though the product of necessity

Her strength

Set the creator at work

After he endorsed and confirmed all good

And welcomed the Sabbaths rest

Her strength

Lured the premiere father

To digress from plan, ate the forbidden

And were repatriates of Eden

Amongst vessels

She is the weaker, still

Her strength-

Have destroyed and kept dreams

Pulled down and built kingdoms

Broken and mould homes... eem, hmm!

No restrictions to its achievements

YOU MADE ME LIVE

They said it's death

You gave it with a smile

With trust I wore

Wear yours

It rules life

Happiness and peace

Red in blood

Red in life

Red is love

Red is life

ASSURED

Up the hill

Sitting near the rushing waters

Heart supporting the jaw

In deep thought

There in deep silence

Suddenly a flash appeared

It looked like an angel

At first glance

Then a jewel, again

An abode to settle in

And my ears opened

The whisper rhyme with

The touch of bliss and gentle rushing waters

When you voice that you love and care

And will be just for me

Worries were gone when

I'm assured you are there

Tears flow from my eyes

Of dream

When I hear you call my name

WOO OF THE RESTRICTED

My heart I give to you

Ensure it didn't fall

It is fragile and could break

The only place to keep it safe

Is in your heart-

For your heart is ever safe

In your inner self

When you can't take it

Give it back to me

If you throw it away

It will break

Give it to someone else

He might be my enemy

And could crush the chest

You can give me yours

I promise to take care of it

To keep it inside mine

And make it safe

Always satisfying you

And make you feel like

A natural diva

BODY LANGUAGE

When my eyes met hers

The once wide-open

Dims wearily

As if I'm narcotic bound

Blinking in assertion

The feel of a young angel-

Vegetation that have

Not known many sojourners

Her practiced steps

Depicts pleas

The plea of availability

As if she is narcotic bound

The dim in her eyes

The sways of her body

The charming frown on her face-

The beckoning

PART 3:
REFLECTIONS

How things that are never imagined
Come into being
In this space

SHARE THE BRIGHTER LIFE- ETIQUETTE

The law of multiplication

Gain as you could covet

But leave baits on your hooks

No privatized seed has ever grown

Be ready to let go

Life is sharing

In sharing is joy of the beneficiary

And more, would the benefactor

Put smile on faces

Then the land would

Send forth the deposited

Equal to the bountiful and sparing

The password of success

ANA EGBU MBE EDOBE OLA?

The best time is now

The perfect timing awaits readiness

Give to today

There is another for tomorrow

In laziness

Are multiple excuses

The fear of adventure eludes

The will for survival and,

The man adjourns his programs

Perhaps never to attempt anymore

Subject to who carries the belt

In the fight

Between will and survival

What withholds the sharing

Of the tortoise

When chiefs abhor the taste?

A weary start

Gradual motivation

Even the dreaded mountain

Is pulled down

PODIUM AND PEWS

All are open

The chances limitless though

Yet limited by attitude

Set whichever

Wherever

All lies on chance

Commitment

And voice

Keeps the podium standing

Reluctance

And sight

Sits on the pews

LIFE

On the sixth day

"Let there be"

Mixed with a task of making

The actors of this theatre

Set to rule and dominate

Coming and going incessantly

The wheels gets recycling

Who is next is never displayed

On any crystal board

Uncertainty abounds and obscurity prevails

Once the step is climbed

Before this step are witnesses

No backing the stage in quietness

Till the exit time

When acts are measured

There is more to life

Than sleeping away the nights

And awaiting the dawn resurgence;

Taking in and out of supplements

Watching every tick by seconds

Activities are run on earth in life

The earlier discovered

The earlier implemented

Life would be fulfilled

To those who exchanged success with convenience

MYTH

What the mind endorses

Nature seem to have no guide

A man's meat may be to another poison

Pitfalls have dug on the plain

One falls and,

Another walks through

The purveyor is belief

The mind the disseminator

Not as common as

All mortal shall demise

In the game which referee is will

A man breathes in and is gone

Another breath and is revived

The referee is the decider

The will of the mind of the man

PUZZLED

No wrong will ever make a right

Not even with baptism though

The heart affirms its actions

Even with the sealed conscience

Which among these could be the truth?

In the scramble for the perfect man

With a common thesis though

Interpretations differs and more confusing

Perhaps each stresses with favor to instilled impunity

Left should be best for the West after all

And right: like a signet sticks to the East

Each becoming their destinations favorite

If the best would be awarded

Save the rival a reputation

That the prize of your crown becomes not

The convenience of others, spent

Nor a fellow's character assassinated

For who among the ever flaw being

Can justify the perfect? If not

The blue print of the secrets of the man- the mind

ELDERS' TALE

How I admire

Sitting at the reminisce and nostalgic

Events of the old

When mum perhaps

Has not been a groom's bride

In nineteen… early twenties

During late eighteen fractions

Down to yore as far as history recorded

Of how beings were traded,

The joys of freedom,

The jubilation of independence,

The dreaded penury of war,

Of the fruit of honesty

And the often betrayal of trust-

To direct the plot

In the acts of life

Having the knowledge of my pre-birth

This makes me "live'"

Beyond when I was born

HEART

Encased in an envelope

Marked never to be seen

Even by the bearer

A world of vagabonds

When the crimson complexion

Runs every affairs of the human race

Sitting in lowly abode of the man

It is not visible though

Her thoughts are objects

And realities

That come and goes

And endures through ages

So dreaded by the gods

Even the God of creation

Seem confused

About whom the heart is-

Subtle than all things

Who can discern it?

CHARACTER

"His is... bad"

"I don't really fancy her..."

They are boring

Like the drops of water

In which below positions

A thirsty can, patiently waiting

Till the gradual feel of the brim is felt

The subconscious man

Made them; feelings that

Once lived in the mind

Which the mouth may have made

To become words

Subtly enticed perhaps

Its first act on stage

Was witnessed by ovation perhaps, that

It pleased habit to tame the once abstract into being

Simplicity confuses most

Gradually the once bound for a test

Enrolled to trait

And fail to resign

Even after much strict measures

RUMOUR

When confusion is born

Sometimes true

Often times an imagination

Perhaps it pleases the ear and

The mouth carried it along

Not a being

Yet is living among human

Without wings it still flies

It travels wider than airplane

Very swift and Skippy

A chameleon of its kind

To some it worth fun

Even when many are devastated

When you perceive it is pleasant

Behold heart break abounds

GESTICULATION

Do I speak?

Who would hold and hear

The defenseless

Left out in the dark-cold

Silence of desolation

Amidst sorrows

Arms-crossing at stoop

But arrow in words pierces still

The bank in the heart lets out moist

As water from a fountain

Through my eyes

Yet the bully vows to torture still

In fear, starving

My bones reflects from her envelope

No confidential is reserved for my members inside

At my glare, in sigh

Sympathizers murmur;

"Where is her mama?"

Often times

Mothers lie at adieu beckoning

And those left are featherless

While the chicks in tender whistle scatters

An offering at the altar

All for the kite to chatter

Enclosed with denial

Like a wingless butterfly

Lying still

Under the soles of the traitor

Scare has tied my mouth

Otherwise I would call for mama

Though she'd read the signs

Before letting her babe struggle

For "survival"

Always feeling the presence of my lord

I would've gestured

To mankind

To find the fault of my form and,

Read the script

That presents this molestation

The child is abused

If the thighs and arms

That once had held

Could hold still

I would gesticulate through my heart though

If they could still understand

The language of our communication

While on her benevolence I laid.

I would gesture the sorrows of the child in labor

She would report my misery

But... what would be my fate?

NOT BECAUSE I'M SOLUBLE

Either with pills

With the piercing of the needle

With prying through in tools

Made on the sixth

And on the seventh the creator rested

Without creatures to praise;

For on the day of my creation

In moist

I poured out

And my complexion was crimson

Flowing across though her thigh

Yet I was not made to evaporate

Dancing the pendulum

Another flow yet

Another evaporate

Creatures-change-crimson

The future breaches

And tomorrow blinks

Is this world different?

Is our world diverse?

Why is my image different?

Oh! My creator

You are built in form

Am liquid

You live

I die

My creator... my killer

I guess

It is not because I'm soluble

For why do creators abound?

Multiplying keen killers

Yet were no gods

If only I was left to will

Who knows...?

I would erase her sigh

I would heal the world

SEIZE... NOW

I'd not seen

But the pricking sadness-

Liable to deafening

The ear heard

Forbidding the eye so chaste

To witness innocent arms

Subscribing to fire arms

And the mind to memorize such trauma

It heard of the spills

Of the crimson falls,

The fall of the Iroko

The plucking of the tender roses

Destruction of erecting sweats

The scramble of the distressed:

As the puzzle of the chess game;

Like the confused runs

Of the inhabitants of a domicile in flames

When unity is ablaze

Peace was in flames

Disappearing to the clouds

So laden

My heart forbid to thud at its tempo

Better not witnessed than described

Had I been then I would evaporate

It wouldn't have been real though

I cherish nature to fault its principle:

A being to assume the fate of heating aqua

Seize now... please

Are you pushed to the wall?

Relax leaning, hear the whispers:

Seize now.

Tackled to the ground?

Taste the ashes of the decomposed

Beckoning: seize now

Pierced in the heart?

Look down to the incarnated crimson once spilled

Look down to the color of love

Singing: seize now

Love

That peace would prevail

JUST FOR THE REST

Delivered twin

The privileges are doubled

Effects are doubled

The initiator- our creator

Fashioned it double

That in attending to the duo

Each has to perform

The sun I shine in the day

The darkness to brighten

For fellow creatures to see

While they toil around

The moon so soothing

Dims in the night

Beautifying my part- darkness

For fellow creatures to rest

After they'd toiled

The remnants of the creatures remain still

Till peacefully we manage our portions

Peace reigning in their minds

The creator at peace

For the creatures peace

PERFORATED WALLS

An abode of confinement

A city which dress code is underwear

A wall with multiple inscriptions-

Most departed sojourners leave finger prints

At the genesis of the visit

Bully perchance welcomes

Then the ambience of memories

The odour of perspiration and secretion

Its quietness is the memories of silence

The shouts- the deprivation of needs and want

The city of resolution and repentance

Hearing sounds of reality but, away from it

Strangers and foes alike

Were made friends and reunite

In sharing and community

Where the good and bad live together

A world where neighbors

Are brothers and friends

Any truth that is obscured here

No jury could investigate

The nights were tripled

Than ordinary nights... outside

How uncomfortable the partitions:

Part 3: Reflections

A little-long sleep

A long awake and, a little slumber

Till the shadow gradually elapses

And another boring day comes up

As weariness ticks uncensored time

In weariness

Ears itches to respond the call of freedom

Uncertainty is the result

Of who' next to depart

Through the protecting barred irons

ONCE GOVERNED

So tempting

But always temporal

Accommodating occupants

Oozing in authority

Prides with power

For the dwellers which tickles

Like the pendulum of time

When seconds are exchanged

Too hot

To approve privatization

It slew predecessors

That bargained its complete acquisition

Therefore guiding the governor

To be governed and,

The once governed

Becoming the governor

Completely spherical

Coming around and going around

Would the governor govern godly?

For the would-govern to be guided

Peace will reign:

Leaving the once governed,

Would govern and,

Never to govern

To enjoy the goodie

Of careful handling of

Human sovereignty

ODE TO THE BLACK MOTHER

So large

She is as old as yore

Standing a colossus

Spreading arms in tender-loving-care

Nursing her roots

Ma'am you inquired of nature

She offered your fruits potentials

In tender-loving-care

You hoarded your fruit

In the Tran Saharan, when the "massas"

Needed a fair share of your talent

To feel the strength in black

Ma'am you lived

When they snatched and forced

Your suckling child from you

You breathed them strength:

To endure but rule their land

Ma'am they survived and are ruling

Beautifying the world in spotted-plain attire

Like the cloud thudded with stars

Your children shone

You redeemed us from penury, hunger, war...

Ma'am

Teach your shepherds

Not to trade the pastures we graze

Making the heir

A slave gracing farther lands for pasture

FIRST LABOUR PER-ANNUM

The last I starred at the LCD

My cell phoned it was thirtieth

Surprises! On another stare at the dawn

It is the first fruit of a thirty-first

Of one-twelfth

Living in three-sixty-five and territory

Realizing from the display-

"LABOUR MONTH"- opted out of configured account

Reminisce flashed back at me

The thriller set some centuries before

How ONE used Judas' noose,

"Law" lifted THREE... in the gallows

"Acquitted" offered mercy' hands to FOUR-

The Broadway as co-script written by

The LABOUR FORCE and EXPLOSION

Only dry lining testified my tears

As my heart sang the tale of:

THE FOUR SIDES OF EIGHT

Personalized presumptions could protest

They had no inclination of explosives

Could their subjects get guts though?

They would counter-

What if some careless cops created

A scene of "Terrorist Attack"

As set in Iraq, Israeli-Hezbollah, and Gaza...

Part 3: Reflections

Slavery burdened labor

However it needed a sacrifice... of blood

To redeem the slave tag with

Servants- possessing some civil rights

Thus:

Fate formed a square

Out of the octagon

The Square went to the gallows

ONE willingly

THREE subjectively

The surviving RECTANGLE

Stretches abroad

Already changed "labour force"

To labour "peacefultsteps"

Peaceful footsteps without... explosives

What a song

With no force though

Its revolution is initiated

By commanding "peacefultsteps"

My mind wonders if,

The dust of "peacefultsteps"

Were still watered

By the arms of power

In this adult century

RESULT ASIDE TRIAL

How we scramble

Uniformed as leaves on green plants

Our purpose to clinch the power of ink

One pulls hard with the gesture

Of a computer file disk though

Another farther, unconcerned, presumes

"Tomorrow determines itself"

Right he may be after all

Everything is possible in...

What is the true test of knowledge?

Examination! Our fathers taught us

Things must have fallen apart

"Monkey dey work, Baboon dey chop"

Answers run together with questions

As pounded yam with *nsalla* soup

One pulls hard again

With the speed of an email

Opening all filed programs

Yet his fate

Lies on the uncertain hands of the examiner

What is the true test of knowledge?

Examination! Nature taught us

Results outside trial

Unusual becoming: what if?

Problems demand solutions directly

Than cunning itself

On the black-spotted white papers

Where the unknown and uncertainty

Determines scores

RAYS OF FLAME

Peeping through the dark

In the middle of the nights

When nature' rested

I saw rays

From the exhausted oil lamp

From the gentle-fast melting wax

The shades, as beautiful as the eclipse

Carving a silhouette of a being

In deep meditation of studies

In a sturdy

I knew his perseverance

I'd engaged with his courage

In broad day

How he's bent on spotted papers

As a goat in grazing grasses

Yet at nights

Refuses to lie

And rest

His goal

A certified accredited seal of success

Behold it around

It's a hurdle, jump over

A sprint, race through

Like a gazelle

Part 3: Reflections

Your success is my pride

Your achievement, my happiness

When the designs

Dotted on white papers

Would appear

I bet you A's

Nature appraise C's

No "Pride" and "Frail"

Would be registered

The designs

When set across the rays

The flame would tilt beautiful colors

Like rainbow

Then with mouth ajar

You would shout:

"Eureka!"

FADED KHAKI

In March

Amidst the soles that marched

Climbing hills

Slopping valleys

The morning drills

The long walks

Later dispersed like seeds

Many in uniform

Facing uniforms

Some in uniform

Meeting mufti masses

Delivering service to the fatherland

In a foreign land

Of the same motherland

Till the dawn of February

Fighting to fly

To soar higher than ever

Such is the joyful expectation

Of the survivors

From an alienated jungle

Soaring high above equals

Faith is the password

Fate would grant

Every service deserves applause

Part 3: Reflections

Ovation would applaud

You'll lead in the labour mart league

The world is waiting

The world needs an answer

Have you...?

Welcome to the world

Hurray!

MASKED STARDOM

Admired by the people

All hail

The eloquent "sweetest voices" with wits of encourager

Gaiety instilled

An inspiration... with the tide of a torrent

Celebrated, so long in the "match box"

That transmits flame through the air

To the world

With a deafening ovation:

I've hit stardom

Surprisingly faceless as a still-mould statute

With the unidentifiable gait

Of a being-parading-masquerade

Even as cheerers guesses- who?

Yet among my admirers

Then I scruple about my status

For prep of, remiss emerged even from my admirers

When face's needed in the showcase

Boon save foible, focal... I would quit

Yet for the love of the flame

Erupting from the "match box"

HARMATTAN

From where are these swaying charcoals?

That drops and stains

Every reflective fabric

And itches the eyes

That tries accommodating it

If the lamb have not been slain

From where is this smoke-cloud?

That moist the eyes

And sneezes every breath

Could these be the smoke of sacrifice?

The steady dizzying wind,

The dried weeds on fire, in the fields

The often-whirled soil,

The always-licked dry lips, announces

The quartet-'ember' months long arrival

The cool breeze

That blows dizziness and

Trance; of how old days have gone and

What impact have made,

Signifies the year' running to rapture

Make me comfortable

Let all my clicks download

My heart will not beat

Before mass returnees-

This harmattan

LABOUR "PAINS"

Suddenly the pains

Were vanished

With the emergence of a new hope, dream-

Uncertain though

Bred from toddler to

Learning language and skills

Wisdom and folly

Facing tomorrow sometimes become awesome

As men in nostalgia

Cherish the good-young-old-days,

That we are tempted

To be as stagnant as a blue lake

Yet we vie for a fulfilled tomorrow

Only courage and focus

Could surpass the distractions

And rigours to success

So long as the moon

Gives way to the sun

One day at a time

Surely we'll emerge

With faith

Or by fate

For then 'friends' and well-wishers

Gathered by your cries, fragrance...

Now your friends gather

Only at your wish

COUNT OF NUMBERS

Just as a foot step counts

In a movement

None, doing without the other

Gradually fulfilling purpose

Seconds becomes minutes and

Hangs in hours

Then all becoming moments

Some cherished

As others are feared

And this one moment- cherished

Such a day as this comes

Once in a life time

Lo! Numbers are counted

As a complete whole

Many more years

Many more moments to cherish

Happy birthday

PICTURE

The duplicate of the original

Most times it lies

Since it is non-living

It detests the progression of reality

The deceiver of its possessors, sometimes

Capitalize on it

Then Laban would give you

Leah for Rachael

The pilot of the journey in to the past

Of the good old days

And travails of bitter past still

A consolation to the departed

Collateral of good bye

Count it among the living

It re-invokes the long forgotten memories

And keeps the long-lost friends and lovers

With stakes among the dead

It' worse than still-birth and

As good as statute

CYBER VILLA

Set on space

Having no speed limit

As movements are in fast-forward

The visitors log in with passwords

Like gestured invitation of

A strictly restricted occasion

A peep

Grants new immigrants fad

And compatriots reason to belong

Like astral travel

Pointing your incantation

On the reflections on the little crystal board

An entrance to the Island on the space

If the air ticket would not be exhausted

The cyber would have citizens

But suddenly it ended like a dream

While the explorer returns

Filled with the villa's flair

If transparency still abides in any city

The internet adorns cyber alike

A knock on any door

Opens access to diverse discipline

A land that nothing is hidden

Even the king's secret

SPOTS ON THE POOL

A dive

Then silence

Alas quietness

Suddenly... the spring

Of life

Like the spark of fountain flow

Lo!

What is thicker than water

Outweighed the aqua and

Defied the force of gravity

If it' an aquatic habitat

The crystal clear liquid

Felt the spots of dead-life

Lying in state

At the executioners chest

THE BLACK BOX

It has wings and could fly

Within, it has temporal

Seats of inhabitation

Its flight is strictly on command

By the absolute control of the tower;

If it's clairvoyant

Perceives no danger ahead

The complexion of the box is

Dark and obscure

The world of the unknown, except

When the lives on board returns

To tell the tale of their joy, woes and travail

Sadly on most black days

When the wings crash

The black box

Hovers in the dark, unseen

And every plot in the scenes

Remains blank with intrigues

And many unresolved questions

LIFE IN LEAVES II

Having made part of

The acre's possessions

Spread in the green, colour of life

Made as though to be vied as vegetation

The world is not on the space

Our roots are firmly pierced in the earthly soil

Nourishing the nostrils

With particles of photosynthesis, inclusive

So long the leaves studs

In the rooted trunk

The studded were many

Of unequal sizes and shapes

And were products of several ages

That departs on diverse times

The sun shines as the wind blows

Plucking at random, the once studded

Making the still-stud lean and wane and pale

Dropping on the earth they wither

And return to their roots

Ahead, their traces may never be reminisce

THE PRICE OF PARADISE

When these hassles are gone

All would subscribe to eternal rest-

Save the scions of perdition-

Rest where joy, peace and thrills

Would thrive

Where no harm would hover

Rather eyes dried from tears

Hearts consoled

For the expectation of the believers

And the hope of the faithful;

Never to be breached

Must be bargained for

Like an experiment

In a science laboratory

Where result' determined by concoctions

Miss one instruction and birth new invention

In the measure of reflex

Biology teaches the power of

Voluntary and involuntary

Which traits would gradually change

From mere conceived thoughts to words

And actions

 Through character

The level only grace would change to leave scars though

My tour to the Deadland

Contrite my heart so hard

Behold the cry of the unborn amongst others

That was forced by caesarian of non-professionals

And burnt right on the second she left the Bellyworld

She cried and beckoned me to stay

Because our world is evil and violent

The scars on this innocent leave nothing but confirmation

As I try to defend my land

An elderly, still in penury

Reflected how he saw burnings beneath,

From aerial view- before they were blown up in a bird's belly

Then I wonder why

The creator would inbuilt explosives on the creature

There were loud cries and wailing still

None recounted their ordeal loudly save in whispers

For phobia of yet another scene

That would cause their second death

With their argument I nearly loved to join them

But only a tourist I was

And my visa expired

The sketches of the suspects were obscured

Like a masked masquerade in the dark

I can't identify the man if I see his picture

They were mere sketches

Done by mere ghosts that are foreigners to canvass

Hear the voice from the repatriate of the Deadland

If you are the man in picture;

I advocate a change

Lest the cry of the innocent blood

Disturb the Almighty to...

Since my return I'd tried to figure

The cause of these wars

Why a faithful would slay a fellow believer

Why a man would kill his brother

If you don't know-

We are one in Abraham

After our tongues were confused in Babel

In the quest to live in paradise prematurely

I guess this paradise have rules

If you'd been to the Caribbean

You would figure the ambience I foresee of it

Yet the paradise supersedes the ambience in the Caribbean

Even the oracles of the Almighty;

Who we advocate for preached peace, love and unity

From whom then do we learn this huge fracas?-

Assuming the visa to the holy city is the color of crimson

I wish I close my eyes and dream

The North and South

The East in the middle and West farther

Pursue a common goal- peace, love and unity

Then our place in paradise would be guaranteed

Then when I return to the Deadland

Maybe as an immigrant to nationalize

I would assure them: the man changed